Why Do Men Rape Often?

By Prasant

Table of Contents

Had the men been descent in the world, girls would have been living a fuller and happier life. But alas, men rape often….why do they do it?

There is the medical science explaining the sexual urge in every male in the society…and that too – of recurring urge. Of course, one won't be satisfied for ever….

Beyond biological explanations, there is a much detailed and highly useful explanation of this category of crime called as 'Rape'…in Numerology.

And it can even predict the rape incidents, trace the hidden rapists.

Numbers Promoting Sexual Urges

Sexual urge is generated by numbers [numerology of the day]. Certain dates carry the 'sex urge/potential' with them. When that date comes, all [including women] feel a strong urge to taste nudity and beyond......and beyond..

Basic numbers which generates sexual urge in us are – Number 5 and Number 6. And when it mixes with number 4 or 8, the crime event occurs.

So, we can say that numbers 4 and 8 promote/pushes one into sexual crimes.

Carrying Within/Event Date

Either the persons in the society are carrying such numbers within themselves [they have their birth dates in 4, 5, 6 and 8 Or born in such periods]

OR ELSE

The event date is in such a number/affected by such numbers -4, 5, 6 or 8. Besides date, it could be in the form of destiny number or other advanced concepts.

The person affected by such numbers are living under danger. Such men might harm innocent girls/ women.

Such girls/ women might indulge in deceitful relations with men, might suffer abuse at the hands of men.

The dates promote this by generating sexual urges in us. On dates 5, 6, there arises a high level of sexual urge in all of us. It is the gift of Nature.

We feel the urge to see the opposite sex in nude state, have mild/strong sexual pleasures with them.

Good people find happiness and relief, on such date, by loving their partners in harmless ways. Evil minded persons resort to RAPES....

Nudism, Group Sex

Nudism, nudity and the concept of group sex [the bad version being gang rapes] comes exclusively from number 5.

When number 5 affects the person or the date, some act of nudity or sex with multiple partners is bound to occur.

All the nude scenes of the various films –hollywood, bollywood, regional are the direct product of number 5.

Check the birth details of those actresses, there will be a 5 without fail. Birth date 5, or added total of full birth date being 5 or born in one of these periods of 5-

May 20- june 27

Aug 20- sept 27

Any person born /affected by number 5 carries the liking for/risk of nudism and group sex during his/her entire life.

AND

Any future date in 5 series – 5, 14, 23..etc carry the potential of nude acts/ group sex in its store. On such dates, somewhere and with someone, such things might be taking place…

Romantic Sex

Number 6 creates the feeling of romance, sex, making the partner pregnant. On such dates, such feelings start developing right from the morning till late night.

Persons [be it a girl or a male] are natural likers of sex in all its sensual forms [right from childhood days till death].

It is natural that girls/ women want it In romantic/good forms, men want it in every form- they resort to rapes too.

Well, this number 6 [date/destiny in number 6 series -6, 15, 24, 33, 42…] might prove as the best tip for those married couples searching the ways to please their partners.

But, not for the unmarried persons!

Prostitution like feel

Number 4 and 8 creates the prostitution like feel. Such dates set the mood for something dirty.

Women/girls born on 8 project around their surroundings- a prostitute like feel [without the awareness of that lady/girl].

Men look at them as potential prostitutes [even though the lady/girl may belong to respectful family, has non-sexy nature/attitude]

Quite naturally, when 4 or 8 mixes with 5/6, it results in sexual crimes of any degree.

Gang Rape date 15

Most of the violent group attacks on girls/ women happen on dates 15. Number 15 is a severe sexy number- it is carrying both, 5 as well as 6…see..

1**5**

15= **6**!

Quite recently, many terrible gang rape attacks have occurred…all on 15th of various months.

Many sensational murder cases traces it crime to date 15 [when we check it in wiki].

Our fatal prediction….

In year 2012, in our website, we had explained 15 and cautioned about gang rape…

And the next month, the horrific gang rape of Indian girl Nirbhaya took place which surfaced on international news too…

Date- 16 dec, 2012

Destiny= 1+6+1+2+2+0+1+2

= **15**

Date and Destiny matrix = 16 plus 15= **31**

Plus Sunday = 31 + 1

32

The four convicts in Delhi gang-rape

Mukesh Singh   Akshay Thakur   Vinay Sharma   Pawan Gupta

www.hindustantimes.com

Child Abuse

This is yet another bad thing and this happens with girls born on number 8 series – dates 8, 17 or 26. Or if her destiny number [added total of one's full birth date] in number 8 series.

Or if, born on the period of 8-

Dec 20-feb 27

Rape Is Surprise Sex

Porn star Sunny Leone says, carelessly, that *'Rape is nothing but a Surprise Sex'*.

But don't you feel, all the pleasures of the rapidly moving muscle, the bursting of semen goes exclusively to the Male…

Imagine the pain and persistent bleeding, burning of raw flesh and your dying body, if your scrotum or a bit of penis gets ripped off accidently.

Is it pleasurable?

Girls, avoid an encounter with men on such dates, most importantly 15 of any month, stay safe….

Aamir [Number 5] Creates Nudity Controversy With PK Poster!

One more number 5 favors nudism, this time it is Aamir khan. We know that persons born under the effect of number 5 likes/publicize nudism without fail.

PK Poster brings male nudity to bollywood in a more appealling form [earlier, it had been attempted by Neil Nitin Mukesh and John Abrahm.

Aamir is looking delicious, no doubt about it. It will certainly enthrall certain sections of the society. Aamir is born mar 14.

These nude scenes of bollywood, hollywood etc are mostly done by actresses affected by number 5 - either birth date, destiny or birth months in one of these two periods-

may 20-june 27

aug 20-sept 27

Few feel it as a social crime..... the viewers mostly enjoy it only.

Sherlyn On Playboy!

Bollywood model/actress Sherlyn Chopra features on the latest issue of adult naked photography magazine Playboy. We will talk about numerology, here too!

Why few girls like nudism ?

You might have seen girls/models in nude photography photos or videos ,even in various ftv shows.Not everyone are forced by circumstances to do such things. Many do it with their own liking. Numerology alone can explain the hidden psychology of such girls.

Girls born in the period of number 5 [april 27 to june 20] and number 6 [aug 27 to october 20] strongly like the concept of nudism and sex.

Even other girls having name components,birth or destiny numbers in 5 or 6 are of bold kind. And same thing applies with birth date or destiny number in number 5 or 6 series.

Number 5 series implies 5, 14, 23, 32, 41, 50, 59..etc. Anything which adds to 5. And number 6 series implies similar thing- 6, 15, 24, 33, 42, 51 etc, anything adding to 6.

Most of the bollywood and hollywood celebrities and other entertainment industries doing nude scenes/sex scenes in films and posing nude for magazines are those affected by the 5 and 6 number category [you can check their birth details in wiki].

Indian actress Mandakini of bollywood film Ram teri ganga maili has a name number in 24 i.e. 6 – who could forget the stir she had created by her famous nude breast feeding scene way back in 1980's !

So, similar is the case with Indian model/actress sherlyn chopra who did the playboy shoot recently.We can't blame them or call them bad !

Sherlyn Affected by 5

Her name itself adds to number 5. Name number, often, shapes our life [with birth date and destiny forming the base].

SHERLYN CHOPRA =

24 + 26 = 50 OR 5!

And the Playboy magazine on which she features has again, the numerology in 5 [most of the adult magazines are 5].

PLAYBOY = 23 OR 5!

[No wonder, the magazine is pushing many many girls towards nudism in exotic manner.]

Latest True Case

'Makadee' Child Artiste Caught Up In Sex Racket Now!

Year 2002 saw National award for best child artiste going to Makadee little girl Shweta Prasad Basu. And now, 12 years later, police has caught her for prostitute business. Her case is yet another example of effects of number 5.

Many complain, argue that it is rude to say that 5 leads to sex, rape etc.. Smashwords is in hot argument with me over my newly released book on the same topic. But, everytime it proves right that number 5 creates the mentality of nudism and sex with multiple partners.

Shweta basu born on jan 11, 1991 fulfills the number 5 critiria, has the affliction by crime number 8 [jan month is 8].And she is carrying on sex racket. Prostitution is nothing but sex with many.

Her destiny number adds to number 23.

In her statement, she confesses that she did it out of poverty. Now, didn't I tell everytime that number 11 creates mental unrest and lack of money? Her birth date is 11.

She says-

"I have made wrong choices in my career, and I was out of money. I had to support my family and some other good causes. All the doors were closed, and some people encouraged me to get into prostitution to earn money. I was helpless, and with no option left to choose, I got involved in this act. I'm not the only one who faced this problem, and there are several other heroines who have gone through this phase."

And more interesting revealation comes....her birth destiny total adds to number 34. This is an unstable number [because 4 tends to become 5]. So, number 35 too was operating in her life. The crime and death number.

National award winning Shweta Basu Prasad was arrested in a high profile prostitution racket in Hyderabad after she was caught red handed with a businessman. The police have also arrested several well-known businessmen along with the her.

Shweta basu prasad also acted in several television shows including Ekta Kapoor's Kahani Ghar Ghar Ki and Karishma Kaa Karishma as a child actor. She was currently working in the Telugu film industry.

It seems that she too had consulted a numerologist for name change...for we see many experiments with her name- Basu added from nowhere, wiki page confused with prasad or basu.

Shweta Basu [the name used for tv/films] added to 24 + 12= 36. The 63 pattern, as always pointed out by us, leads to bad names, downfall. She is in her 24th age!

More articles and help –

Prasantnair1@gmail.com

Other books by the same author-

Why Did I Commit Suicide?
[Kindle Edition]

https://www.amazon.in/dp/B00N4OP1RG

Why Do Men Rape Often?
[Kindle Edition]

Philip Hoffman's Death
[Kindle Edition]

Prasant Numerology

A short journey through the concepts and methods of Prasant Numerology – the beginner's guide.

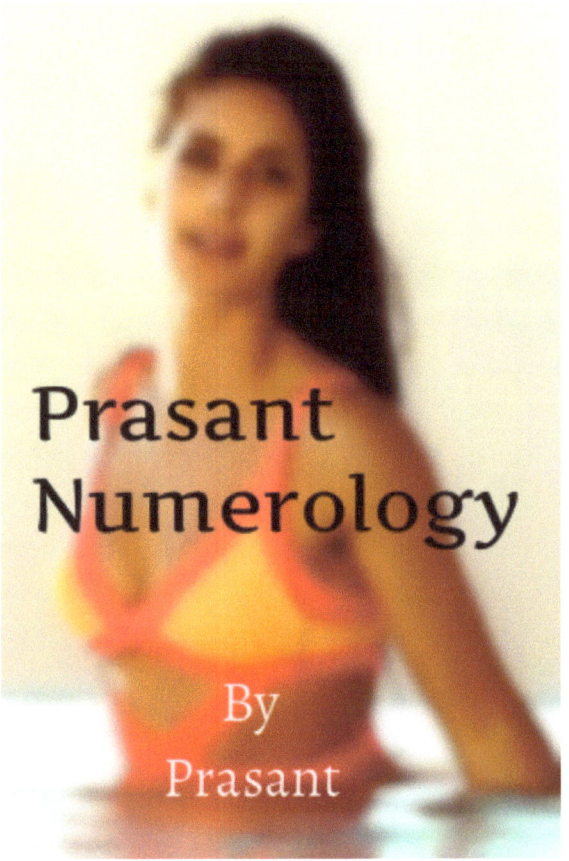

https://www.smashwords.com/books/view/472234

Suchitra Sen' Death Code
[Kindle Edition]

Tried our death decoding numerology on actress Suchitra Sen. Her numbers were strongly hinting at her nearing death....Our prediction turned true........

http://www.amazon.in/gp/product/B00HWR4T2E

www.ingramcontent.com/pod-product-compliance
Lightning Source LLC
Chambersburg PA
CBHW040318010626

45792CB00023B/1006